Maryland
IN FOCUS

PHOTOGRAPHY AND TEXT BY MIDDLETON EVANS

MIDDLETON PRESS   BALTIMORE, MARYLAND

International Standard Book Number: 0-9620806-0-8

Library of Congress Catalog Card Number: 88-090977

Copyright ©: Middleton Evans, 1988

Book Design: Middleton Evans

Printer: The Sheridan Press • Hanover, Pennsylvania

Color Separations: GraphTec • Baltimore, Maryland

Bindery: Advantage Book Binding • Glen Burnie, Maryland

Publisher: Middleton Press • 7801 York Road—Suite 145
        Baltimore, Maryland • (301) 821-1090

First Edition, Second Printing 1989

DEDICATION

To My Parents
and Sister

CONTENTS

Above: Maple sap is gathered at a Garrett County farm.
Page 1: Vacationers enjoy sunrise over the Atlantic Ocean.
Page 2: Yachts compete in a race off of Annapolis.
Page 3: Oysters are hauled aboard the skipjack Rebecca T. Ruark.
Pages 6–7: Ocean City is inundated on a July Fourth weekend.
Page 13: A guard relaxes at Fort McHenry in Baltimore.
Pages 14–15: Morning mist rises over a Baltimore County horse farm.

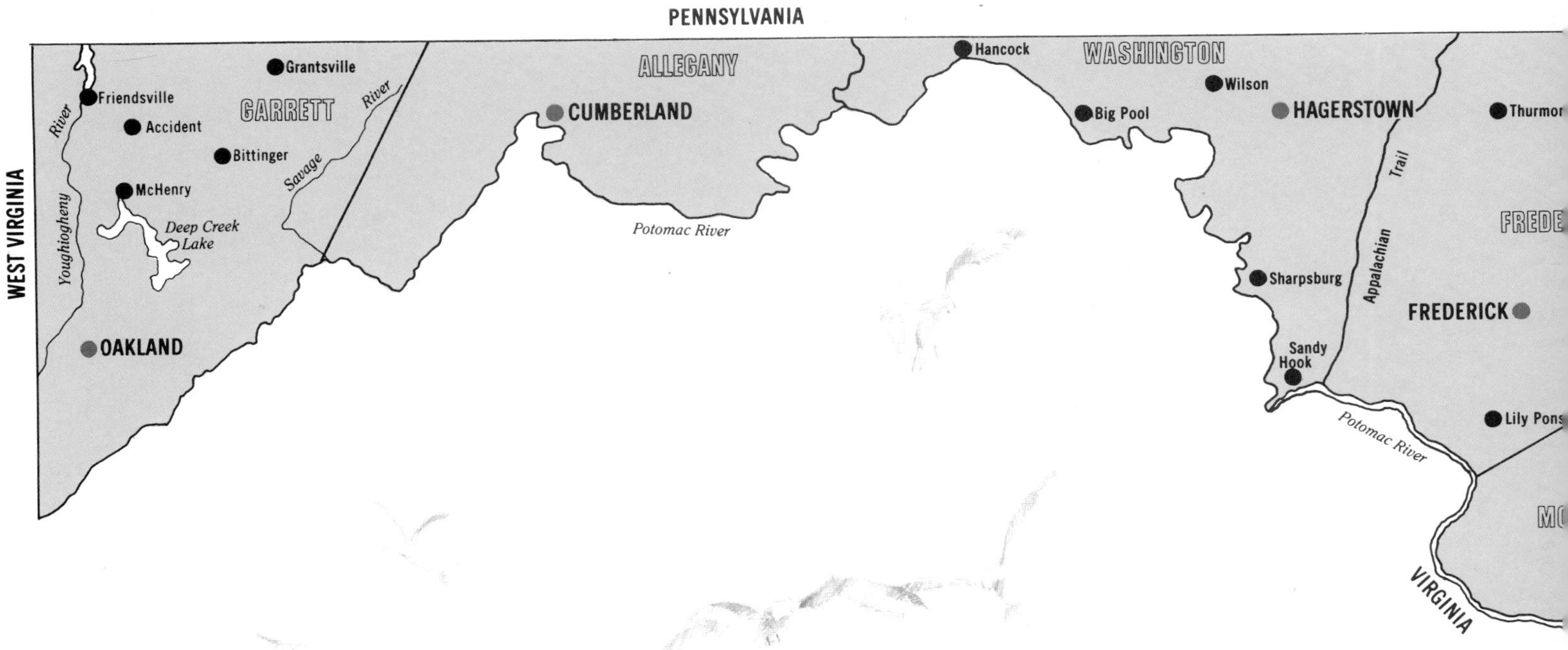

WEST VIRGINIA

ALLEGANY

WASHINGTON

Hancock

Wilson

● Grantsville

GARRETT

● Friendsville

● Accident

● Bittinger

● CUMBERLAND

● Big Pool

● HAGERSTOWN

● Thurmor

● McHenry

Deep Creek
Lake

Savage River

Youghiogheny River

Potomac River

Appalachian Trail

● Sharpsburg

FREDE

FREDERICK

● OAKLAND

Sandy
Hook

● Lily Pons

Potomac River

VIRGINIA

MO

MARYLAND

INTRODUCTION

Maryland. "More Than You Can Imagine." "Land of Pleasant Living." "America in Miniature." What more can be said about the diversity and appeal of my home state? As a skeptic who adheres to "seeing is believing," I set out to see for myself if such generous descriptions are appropriate. After two years of exploration, I am amazed by Maryland's wealth of traditions, scenery, and distinctions. This book is intended not just to document, but to celebrate Maryland.

On graduating from college in May 1986, I challenged myself to assemble this photographic essay about Maryland. When friends asked me what the book would cover, I would describe the Maryland I knew, and the distinguishing features I planned to capture in photographs. High priority would be given to Annapolis, our famed colonial city and capital, sailing mecca of the East Coast, and home to the United States Naval Academy; and to Baltimore, the great port city renowned for its diverse cultural life, institutions, and revitalized Inner Harbor; and to Ocean City, our summer playground. Another dominant theme would be the Chesapeake Bay, home to thousands of boating enthusiasts, many species of waterfowl, delights to the palate such as the blue crab and oyster, and the watermen who harvest these and other riches of the bay. Certainly horses, especially the Preakness and the Maryland Hunt Cup, the spring ritual of lacrosse, and the tobacco industry were also a must in a portrait of Maryland. Historic landmarks and celebrations of the Free State's rich and colorful heritage could not be overlooked. Not to forget the ever-changing moods of the land—these subjects were the essence of Maryland to me.

Yet during my exploration and photography, I came to realize that there was much more to Maryland than my twenty-four years of living here had revealed. Hidden within the fabric of traditional Maryland was an exciting mixture of surprises which came to light only upon searching for them. "America in Miniature" is more than just a catchy nickname. Sometimes I would hear about, or stumble upon, scenery and traditions that seemed more closely associated with New England, the South, or the West than with a Middle Atlantic state. Other times I felt as though I was just in America, no place specific, but nowhere else. Another surprise for me was the range of annual events held throughout the state, celebrating everything from wine and waterfowl to the Renaissance and Polish heritage. On the whole, it seemed almost unfair for such a small state to be so gifted.

* * * *

Originally, my research simply involved looking back through the seasons of the year and reminiscing about growing up in Maryland. Summer, with its two lasting symbols, crabs and Ocean City, was always my favorite time of year. I learned at an early age how to swiftly pick apart the intimidating blue crab; if you are not quick enough you do not get your share at the family crab feast. Before long, disassembling this creature is no more offensive than breaking a roll in half, but it is usually difficult to convince an out-of-town guest that it is really not unpleasant.

(Speaking of crabs, I used to enjoy passing by Phillips Crab House in Ocean City and looking to see how long the line was; as I recall, the wait was always worth it.) The beach is another delight of growing up in Maryland. As a child I found Ocean City to be a magical world of new sensations: scorching sand and frigid water, chewy saltwater taffy, screaming aboard a roller coaster plunging to the earth, aromatic tanning lotions, and the hissing of a kite struggling in a stiff afternoon breeze. My favorite family adventure was riding those rickety old bicycles up and down the boardwalk after a good breakfast; I can still hear the boards creaking under the strain. As an adult, I find that the beach still retains its charm, and it also offers sights that were previously unappreciated. Other summertime memories focus on the Chesapeake Bay. The best way to enjoy the bay is aboard a boat. For several years our family had a powerboat for fishing. Though we rarely caught fish in those fertile waters, watching all the sailboats, and occasionally a Tall Ship, somehow made up for it. No fun-filled summer was complete without a trip to the Maryland State Fair in Timonium. Farm animals were my favorite attraction, but walking to the Cow Palace meant passing through the games arcade; I never liked the heckling by the vendors, but I figured they were just doing their jobs. There never seemed to be enough time to enjoy all of the rides, taste all of the food, and view all of the animals. Perhaps that is why I never grew tired of the State Fair. A final summer memory—every seventeen years (so far twice in my life) we are invaded by the hoards of cicadas which strike especially hard in Maryland. Suddenly we were living in a world dominated by their presence, and all we could do was count down the days until the ground reclaimed them.

As I look back, Autumn was the most dramatic time of year because of its spectacular foliage. Though I have often wondered what New England looks like at this time of year, Maryland autumns leave little to the imagination. Scenic drives around horse country with my father were always highly anticipated. Another ritual of fall was a long walk in the woods, and no trip to the countryside was complete without sweet, crunchy apples from one of the numerous roadside produce stands.

In winter I enjoyed excursions to the Eastern Shore, in search of waterfowl. Though birds could be found all over the region, my favorite spot was Blackwater National Wildlife Refuge, located twelve miles south of Cambridge, where I could count on seeing scores of Canada geese, mallards, great blue herons, tundra swans, snow geese, and an occasional bald eagle. Winter is snow, and since it snows sparingly in Maryland, a good snowfall was all the more exciting, especially for a child who did not have to worry about driving in it. I can still remember sitting by the window, entranced by the relentless falling of the flakes, and hoping that there would be enough to close school.

As I grew up in Baltimore, I found Spring to be synonymous with three occasions. First and foremost is the Maryland Hunt Cup, which is as much a social occasion as a sporting event. While more civilized adults preferred a tailgating party, teenagers would celebrate in less sophisticated ways. Yet come post time all spectators claimed their hillside perches to watch the dots criss-cross Worthington Valley, in the heart of Baltimore County's horse country. As this race is the most difficult steeplechase in the country, not all jockeys make it to the finish line, but those

who do often treat the crowd to an exciting finish. Just around the time of the Hunt Cup, Sherwood Gardens, in northern Baltimore, is peaking in an explosion of color. To me, people enjoying the gardens are just as interesting a spectacle as are the flowers. On a warm weekend the famed gardens are packed. At least a dozen family portraits are in the making at any given time, frisbees are flying, dogs are going crazy over all of the commotion, cameras are clicking away, and there is always a handful of lovers, oblivious to it all. Finally, Spring means lacrosse, which is more than just a sport at which we Marylanders excel; it is practically a way of life. For a Baltimorean, the ultimate display of this "fastest game on foot" is the frequent champion Johns Hopkins University Blue Jays racking up goals at Homewood Field. All these memories had a big influence on my selection of subjects for the book, but they were just a starting point.

* * * *

Realizing that my knowledge of the state was limited to my own personal experiences, I began to read about the state to learn more. Among the impressive array of publications on Maryland, several have been especially helpful to me. Concerning the well-documented Chesapeake Bay, William W. Warner's *Beautiful Swimmers* provides a colorful analysis of the watermen and the inscrutable blue crab. For an overview of the state's variety of people and places, I have enjoyed *Maryland Lost and Found* by Eugene L. Meyer. Another valuable resource has been *Maryland* magazine, which covers everything from the economy and science to history and nature. Much to my surprise, I found that I knew little about Baltimore and even less about Maryland's remote counties. I never imagined that there were so many points of interest throughout the state. Though I have been unable to capture all of these highlights, as the book would be too big, I have tried to capture enough to reveal the distinct mood and character of each part of the state.

Visiting the Eastern Shore is like stepping back in time, especially in the less traveled parts. The best example of old-time America is Smith Island, a unique island community several miles out in the bay. I visited there three times, via the daily mail boat, and learned that there is no local government, law enforcement, or doctor, and the streets do not have names. Besides houses, the only buildings in the island's three towns are churches, post offices, general stores, a fire house, and a school. Life is simple there. Driving through Southern Maryland is also like going back in time, but with a southern flavor. I will never forget my first glimpse of the region: colorfully-garbed field workers hunched over in a hot tobacco field; the atmosphere was very heavy. Even more impressive was a tobacco auction at the Hughesville warehouse in Charles County. Here farmers spoke in an accent which seemed to be more characteristic of North Carolina than of Maryland. I was anxious to capture the atmosphere on film, but my tension could only hint at that of these proud farmers, whose reward for months of hard work in the fields was about to be determined by the highest bids. The sense of history in Southern Maryland is inescapable, especially when horse-drawn buggies frequently pass by; the region is home to large Amish and Mennonite communities. I am also impressed with the pride in

history, which is highlighted by historic St. Mary's City, along the banks of the Potomac River. Here life in seventeenth-century Maryland is meticulously portrayed in a variety of exhibits.

Central Maryland is a fascinating blend of the past and the present. While listening to a park ranger at Baltimore's Fort McHenry discuss how Francis Scott Key wrote the words to the *Star-Spangled Banner* during the British attack on the fort, I was struck by the sight of a container ship juxtaposed against the massive infrastructure of the Bethlehem Steel plant on Sparrows Point. Such contrasts are commonplace in Central Maryland. Downtown Baltimore offers a vast array of concrete, steel, and glass designs, all pushing towards the sky. Just an hour's drive to the south is Annapolis, which has more original Colonial buildings than any other city in the nation. Beyond the suburban sprawl of the Baltimore-Washington corridor are glimpses of classic rural America. There are numerous opportunities to sample a taste of country life. One such place is the Carroll County Farm Museum in Westminster, which hosts special events like the Deer Creek Fiddlers Convention. Central Maryland is also Maryland's famous horse country. Finally, Western Maryland takes on the mood of Appalachia, as there are areas in need of economic development. Yet this mountainous area has a rugged spirit, inviting to those who love the great outdoors. My most exciting adventure in Western Maryland was whitewater rafting along a twelve-mile stretch of the Youghiogheny River. There are a series of tough rapids which make the experience unforgettable.

* * * *

I received my first camera when I was ten years old. For about five years the hobby involved no more than packing away my Kodak Instamatic in the suitcase. Then one Christmas I graduated to a 35mm SLR camera. I felt that my pictures were beginning to improve as I had numerous opportunities to photograph interesting subjects while traveling with my parents. The hobby slowly became a passion. I was easily inspired by the photographs in *Life, Audubon,* and *National Geographic* magazines. Most inspirational, however, were the books of A. Aubrey Bodine, Maryland's most famous photographer, who had an uncanny ability to integrate subjects and their environment, achieving a painterly quality. If this man could create such masterpieces in Maryland, then maybe this state would be a good place to practice. Thus I took every opportunity to photograph during breaks from high school and college; several shots from these excursions appear in this book.

Though observation of exceptional photography has been my only education in photography, I do not feel deprived in any way. My only frustration, however, was the lack of opportunity to develop and improve my skills. My big chance finally came during my junior year of college, when I studied abroad at the University of London. As the academic requirements for exchange students were less demanding than those of my program at Duke University, I rejoiced at the freedom to pursue my craft in such a magical place as Great Britain. During this period of almost daily photography sessions, my tastes expanded from nature and landscapes to people, which is now my favorite subject. By the end of the experience, photography was so much in my blood that I could not resist it, despite my education in economics and business.

Steady shooting has taught me as much about photography as it has about Maryland. From the outset I committed myself to going all out on every assignment, and I was willing to make any sacrifice to capture subjects at their best. A handful of the pictures came easily, whereby I stumbled upon a subject and all of the elements fit together. Unfortunately, most of the photographs required a lengthy process of research, scouting, and repeated attempts at the shot until the moment was right. Peak moments are few and far between, but I have never known a feeling more exhilarating than getting the shot upon making the necessary sacrifices. After waiting twelve hours, over three days, I finally captured a wild bald eagle at Blackwater National Wildlife Refuge. Every hour I wanted to quit, but when the eagle soared over my head and landed on his favorite perch, I knew the wait was worth it. Similarly, I had to carry heavy camera equipment up an ice-covered mountain at Wisp Ski Area (much to the amusement of skiers on the lift above) to capture the atmosphere of downhill skiing. Every thirty yards I had to stop for lack of breath, but I made it to the top, and unfortunately, I decided to do it all over again the next day, as the weather conditions were better.

The most important lesson I learned is that good photography requires one thing more than infinite patience and common sense. Desire is the key ingredient. Put quite simply, if I do not get a shot that has been planned for, then I did not want it badly enough. One of my most difficult assignments was Ladew Topiary Gardens, which I was anxious to include after learning of its national recognition. When I visited one fall afternoon, I did not see any dramatic angles, but I thought about it awhile and decided that a snowfall scene would do the gardens justice. Since the grounds are closed to the public in winter, I first had to get special permission to make the shot. Then came the difficult part: waiting. Two months passed before a big storm hit, and I set out the next morning for this pocket of Victorian England in Harford County. The journey was hazardous, as my light car was getting stuck everywhere, but I could not turn back. Eventually I made it, only to find the front gates locked; the snow was deep enough to keep the staff at home. While trying to figure out what to do, I noticed a movement on the grounds. Fortunately, it turned out to be a caretaker who lived there, and he kindly admitted me to the winter wonderland.

If there is one event that I could not afford to miss, it would have to be the Maryland Hunt Cup. After carefully claiming my spot hours before, the motor drive on my camera jammed a few minutes before the start of the race. I had never experienced this malfunction before, and I did not know how to fix it. Fortunately, I had brought along as a backup an expert from my favorite camera shop, and he knew exactly what to do.

Once in a while I set up a shot so well that I feel nothing can go wrong, and that is usually when the unexpected happens. Most beach-goers who are familiar with the Best Body on the Beach Contest are also aware of the Miss & Mr. Ocean City Contest. As enthusiasm for this popular competition is great, I was anxious to cover it. To get the proper angle I first had to purchase a stepladder to enable me to shoot over the heads of the spec-

tators. Three hours before the finals during Labor Day weekend I claimed my predetermined spot on the beach and waited. The light was right, and I was quite pleased with the situation. With twenty minutes to go, and the beach packed, a couple right in front of the stage stood up on a pair of chairs to get a better view. My blood pressure soared as their heads were now in my frame. Immediately I made my way through the crowd and politely asked them if they would stand on the beach with everyone else. Much to my surprise they totally ignored me, even after explaining that they were obstructing a shot for a publication. Fortunately, I found a security guard and convinced him to correct the situation.

The most demanding assignment of the project was photographing ospreys at close range. From the outset I had planned to include these magnificent birds, symbols of the vitality of the Chesapeake Bay environment. There are hundreds of nests throughout the area, but only a handful are well situated for photographers; I hoped to find one such nest. Several months of scouting passed before a friend informed me of a nest located just ten yards off of a pier along the Chester River. The site proved to be perfect, but unfortunately the birds flew away when I approached. I was too late. I soon learned that the best time to photograph ospreys is early June, when the chicks have just hatched. Another eleven months of waiting. The following spring I assembled a blind, tracked down and rented an extremely powerful telephoto lens, and set up at the end of the pier. Though the mother and newly-hatched chicks did not mind my presence, the father was reluctant to return to the nest. On several occasions he approached the nest, began his descent, and backed off at the last instant. Fortunately, the instinct to carry out parental duties prevailed. He finally landed, dancing in the air with powerful wing strokes, and a fish grasped in vise-like talons; then I knew that my aspirations of two years were finally realized. There are stories behind most of the photographs in this book, and they are vivid testimony to my belief that any photograph is obtainable provided that the desire is there.

*   *   *   *

In conclusion, I have set out not just to show what Maryland looks like, but more importantly to provide the reader with a feel for Maryland lifestyles. The range of cities and towns, history and culture, natural scenery, recreational opportunities, and people is so impressive that I felt Maryland deserved a book where every effort was made to capture subjects at their best. For those who live here, relive classic Maryland memories and expect the unexpected. For those who want to know more about Maryland, I offer this collection for their enlightenment and pleasure.

Middleton Evans
June 1, 1988

THE EASTERN SHORE

The Eastern Shore of Maryland has often been referred to as the land that time forgot. Stretching from Cecil County in the north, the region follows the Chesapeake Bay southward to form a diamond of tidewater counties shaped over the millennia by the sand deposits of the Susquehanna River. Until recently, the Eastern Shore was isolated from the commercial and political mainstream of Maryland and few outsiders settled in its tightly knit communities. Pride of birth and heritage prompted local citizens to boast that "a hundred years ain't a very long time on the Eastern Shore!" Three states, Delaware, Maryland, and Virginia, have sovereignty on the Eastern Shore; and the name Delmarva (as the region is popularly referred to) testifies to the political allegiance of its inhabitants. Most residents identify more with the region as a social entity than with its hyphenate political structure.

Today the Chesapeake Bay Bridge spans connect metropolitan Maryland with this vast history-soaked agricultural region. The Eastern Shore is a flat coastal plain. Nowhere on the Shore does elevation reach 100 feet. If you fly over the Atlantic seaboard between Boston and Richmond, you will be struck by the simple fact that the Eastern Shore is the last major green space left in this megalopolitan strip. It is a land of pine and honeysuckle, a land of fields loaded with corn, grain, and truck produce. The marine climate of Chesapeake Bay makes winters mild; and temperatures rarely plunge below the freezing mark. Summers are ferociously hot and humid, almost subtropical in nature. It is a rainy climate, the region averaging about two inches of rain a month. Thunderstorms in summer are frequent and fierce.

It is the kind of climate that encourages loafing, hunting, fishing, and general revelry. For Eastern Shoremen, happiness is to run into a school of "blues" while fishing on a lazy summer day or to savor the deep dark red skies of a summer sunset. The region does little to encourage moral or philosophical speculation.

To waterfowlers throughout America, the Eastern Shore is known as a goose and duck hunter's paradise. Nature and man are on an even footing here, and the region tests a hunter's skill like no other in Maryland. Each year Maryland's Eastern Shore attracts over 60,000 waterfowl hunters during the 70-day Canada goose season. With over 700,000 migratory Canada honkers wintering in the Chesapeake, goose hunting is so good on the Shore that *Sports Afield* magazine has given it its own sobriquet, "an American classic." In November, when the sky on the Shore turns dark gray and the mists seep up from the salt marsh on to the farm lands, you can hear the piercing noises of thousands of honking geese. It is that wild call of migrating birds that stirs a man's blood and sense of wonder.

The Eastern Shore is also the home of the Chesapeake waterman. Using skills and techniques of harvesting oysters, crabs and fish from the bay that have remained relatively unchanged over the centuries, the waterman is one of the most picturesque and envied regional figures. Out on the bay there are no bosses or time clocks, only man and nature. The waterman is envied because he is a free spirit on the Chesapeake, though few stop to contemplate the grueling labor that is part of the waterman's everyday life. Boats have to be maintained, oyster rakes and crab pots repaired, the weather can turn against you, and crab and oyster harvests may be lean. To be a Chesapeake Bay waterman is to work from sunup to sundown.

The term "waterman" was used in sixteenth-century England to describe waterborne taximen who carried Englishmen up and down the Thames. A hundred years later when the first English settlers reached the Eastern Shore they found a waterland that was rich in fish, crabs, oysters and clams and the term waterman took on a new meaning. Today on Smith Island you can still discern the slight traces of Elizabethan accent that connects the island watermen to their colonial ancestors.

Recently watermen have suffered economically because of declining oyster harvests. MSX, a dreadful oyster parasite, has decimated oyster bars and has forced watermen to rely primarily on crabs and fish to maintain their livelihood. Also pollution and urban development threaten the ecology of the bay and endanger the waterman's livelihood.

Yet, on a brilliant late November day when the skipjack fleet leaves its harbor in Wenona to begin its annual cycle of dredging for oysters, it is difficult not to feel a sense of awe and respect for these Chesapeake men. Once there were over a thousand of the single-masted sailing oyster dredge boats. Now there are less than a handful that continue to work in the oyster industry. The skipjacks are as much a declining species as are the oysters they harvest.

Most visitors to the Eastern Shore see little beyond Route 50. They speed across the landscape in pell-mell rush to get to the resort of Ocean City. Thus it is to the good that Route 50 carries tourists through some of the most scenic farm land in the state. Late in summer the fields are bulging with corn; and roadside stands offer delicious fresh produce that only minutes earlier lay in the fields. In the autumn, the fields of the Eastern Shore are bright orange with the harvest of thousands of pumpkins which soon will be turned into Halloween jack-o-lanterns all over the state.

Ocean City strides Worcester County's barrier island on the Sinepuxent Bay like a modern neon and steel colossus. In midsummer the resort is jam-packed with hundreds of thousands of tourists who have come to play in the surf, join charter fishing parties, and unwind from a year's labor. At night the boardwalk becomes a panorama of humanity strolling, gawking, eating french fries and lining up for rides at the amusement parks. Ocean City is famed for its bathing beauties and each year sunworshippers flock to the resort to enter Ocean City's "Best Body on The Beach" contest.

Ocean City offers a bold counterpoint to the more sedate and quotidian habits of the Eastern Shore. But it is part of a region that has captured the imagination of a metropolitan hinterland of nearly 12 million Americans. Whether it's surfing at Ocean City, hunting geese in Kent County, or walking through a rich harvest field in Caroline County or hunting for crabs in the shallow waters of Tangier Sound, there is something for everyone on Maryland's Eastern Shore.

John R. Wennersten is Professor of U.S. History at the University of Maryland—Eastern Shore.

CENTRAL
MARYLAND

When the Almighty and the elements created piedmont Maryland, they certainly knew what they were doing. Give them plenty of fish and fowl, the program read, and so it was—a cornucopia of foodstuffs for virtually nothing, free to the Indians and then to fishermen, watermen and hunters, and in vast numbers like the 100 million or so bushels of oysters that used to come out of Chesapeake Bay a century ago.

So rich, in fact, was the Central Maryland countyside in teeming wildlife that it nearly frightened Captain John Smith as he sailed up the bay in 1608, and the captain was not an easy man to scare.

Today, that landscape is deeply altered. The giant and impenetrable forest of 400 years ago, avoided even by Indians, is gone. It was a V-shaped thicket that pointed downward through the state to the mouth of the Patapsco River, centering on what is now Baltimore City and County. In its place is a region of intense contrasts.

One of the world's larger science and technology centers has sprouted along the rolling uplands of Prince George's and Montgomery counties. Housing has thundered through outer suburbs of major centers and has reached the environs of county capitals like Hagerstown, Westminster and Frederick. The region is now the bottom end of the Bosh-Wash "megalopolis," the rail and road-threaded megacity said to be clearly visible from the moon.

Only Central Maryland's climate has remained roughly the same. Sharp and sometimes violent changes in its well-watered profile are the rule. The humidity has the side effect of giving middle Maryland a great variety of light values, richly wavering tones that are a creative challenge to painters and photographers.

Things happen that are visual drama. Low-lying morning fog makes the valley meadows of the piedmont counties mysterious. Vast, operatic cloud masses move in continually from the west, giving the whole fall line district perhaps the state's most spectacular sunsets, raying down on farmland and blazing behind the mini-mountains of the Blue Ridge.

Equally sensuous and musical is the level, sunrise quality of the central wetlands, Anne Arundel and Harford counties' river and bay world, and parts of southern Baltimore county, also. Here water and reflected warmth shape the tones of life. Everything shimmers.

The static, abstract sense of the American far west is missing. In its place is hourly change and the response of greenery. A long, cool spring in Maryland can dazzle with its spectacular pink and white floral bombardments from floral trees, wild cherry, dogwood, orchard apples, peaches, locust trees and rhododendron.

Such natural joys punctuate Maryland suburbia. Washington and Baltimore sprawl is there but so are crossroads villages that have changed little in 150 years, plus entirely new civic formations on the land. An example is the planned city of Columbia, a Howard County mecca that expresses twentieth-century suburban longings with as accurate a beat as nearby Ellicott City displays the tumbling romance of a nineteenth-century milltown.

Baltimore's white steps express still another American living pattern, closepacked row homes built near factory centers and made affordably modest for the days of $1 a day workmen. Picturesque neighborhood enclaves with "old country" churches near most doorsteps grew up along with folk art forms.

One looks at Central Maryland sometimes and wonders why so much of it is still left—northern Baltimore County's gorgeous hunt country, central historic Annapolis and the great piedmont farm district from the Susquehanna to Great Falls on the Potomac. After all, through this district pass four major highways and the heaviest traveled railroad line in the world and the majority of U.S. tourists, also, to say nothing of most foreign callers.

I think the answer lies embedded in planning. First came the plan for Washington City. In the late nineteenth century and later, Baltimore vibrated with planned communities, Guilford, Roland Park, Sudbrook Park and Northwood. In the 1930s, the government planned and executed Greenbelt as a federal town under auspices of the New Deal. Today the state can claim to be one of the planning centers of the western world with firms like the Rouse Company and RTKL, Inc., famed for reshaping and adapting the nation's structural heritage.

Planning cannot, however, wholly explain the environmental plusses of much of Central Maryland, an area where things are not large, as in the West and South, or truly small, as in New England. There is something about the variety of life and land that enriches. The scale of things works.

Why is it that the giant Bay Bridge, four miles long, fails to overwhelm tiny eighteenth-century Annapolis? Even with forty story buildings on its shoreline, Baltimore's Inner Harbor maintains a pedestrian intimacy, a human scale. Minutes away from the roaring roadways of I-95 or I-83 one can find hundreds of coves and enclaves little changed since the eighteenth century.

There is no single answer for the survival. The fact is that Central Maryland, never remote, swept by the currents of the Civil War, a busy arsenal for that one and the two great wars of the twentieth century, seems to have come through with most of its traditions untattered and its land still lovely and loved.

Carleton Jones is a Baltimore Journalist and Historian.

SOUTHERN MARYLAND

Southern Maryland is not a clearly-defined geographical area. It is a concept, a configuration, a somewhat elusive entity whose boundaries have shifted in the course of the last three hundred years. As recently as 1914, when the Southern Maryland Society was created, Southern Maryland was described as comprising five counties: St. Mary's, Anne Arundel, Calvert, Charles, and Prince George's. Now the consensus is that Southern Maryland consists of the three southernmost counties: Calvert, Charles, and St. Mary's. They are situated on the peninsula bounded by the Chesapeake Bay on the east and by the Potomac River on the south and west. Two great rivers, the Potomac and the Patuxent, flow through this land. No part of Southern Maryland is more than a few miles from navigable waters; hence, the sense of water permeating the whole place, is one of Southern Maryland's most typical features.

Each of the three Southern Maryland counties is diversified in landscape and beautiful in its own right. Calvert is arguably the finest jewel in Southern Maryland's triple crown, because its landscape is, so far, the least disfigured as a result of the seemingly uncontrollable invasion of former urban residents fleeing the overcrowding of the encroaching megalopolis. Solomons Island in Calvert County is the quintessential water resort. It is also the unusual phenomenon of a Southern town increasingly glittering with East Coast sophistication. The place has a pronounced maritime flavor that feels like being at sea on land. Fronting both the Chesapeake Bay and the Patuxent River, Solomons Island typifies the predominantly nautical configuration of Southern Maryland and is a boat building and fishing center, as well as the birthplace of the skipjack.

Southern Maryland has picturesque country roads, winding through forests of oak, walnut, and pine, especially in St. Mary's County. Rolling hills, peaceful farmland, serenely beautiful country estates with stately homes reminiscent of the English countryside, alternate to charm the eye and soul of the beholder. Some seventeenth-century homes, meticulously restored and preserved, that can still be found in Southern Maryland, have been occupied on a continuous basis for the last three centuries by the descendants of the early settlers who built them. Lovely churches and ancient cemeteries, shrouded in mist and mystery, fields of green tobacco leaves, and red barns outlined against deep blue skies, are some of the colorful elements that form the unique pattern of this land. Motorists driving along the roads that border Southern Maryland's larger estates, can catch, in some of them, glimpses of thoroughbred horses grazing in rolling green pastures, with fillies and colts chasing each other in spirited play that delights even the most casual observer. Horse racing and horse breeding were introduced in Maryland in the early part of the eighteenth century by Benjamin Tasker, a prominent Calvert Countian, and are still part of the local way of life.

The history of Maryland as a whole began in its southern section, with the arrival of the *Ark* and the *Dove* and the landing of the first settlers at St. Clement's Island in St. Mary's County. The region enjoyed a slow-paced, leisurely way of life for the better part of the last three centuries, with the exception of the War of 1812, which brought fire and destruction to several homes and townships along the Patuxent River. The battles of the Revolutionary War and the War Between the States were fought elsewhere. The wounds inflicted by the latter tore many hearts and families asunder, but the landscape was unaffected. Electrification and the automobile culture brought waves of irreversible change to Southern Maryland's tranquil shores. The establishment of naval bases and training centers during World War II in St. Mary's and Calvert counties somewhat altered their physical and social environments. Other human and non-human agencies contributed to changing Southern Maryland's landscape. Many of the trees that had managed to grow back after the first deforestation onslaught at the hands of the early settlers, were sacrificed to serve the interests of today's ultimate destroyer, the ubiquitous developer. Fortunately, many oases of unspoiled beauty and houses gracefully attuned to the natural environment remain to comfort our eyes and soul, together with one of Southern Maryland's most charming features, its old churches. Some of the most attractive churches still in existence were built by the Jesuits, whose members played a role in the early settlement of the Maryland colony similar to that played by the Pilgrim Fathers in the Plymouth colony in Massachusetts. St. Ignatius at Hilltop (aptly named for its scenic location) in Charles County and St. Ignatius on St. Inigo's Manor in St. Mary's county exemplify one type of church architecture, while Christ Church and Middleham Chapel in Calvert County, restored to their simple seventeenth-century elegance, remind Southern Marylanders of the early Puritans' ability to combine beauty and functionality.

Middleton Evans has captured in his artistic compositions the unique quality of Southern Maryland's landscapes, seascapes, and skyscapes. Above all, his images are bathed in the delicate, shimmering light imparted to the air by the ubiquitous water element. He has also focused his magic camera on the faces of the people of Southern Maryland at work and play. Some of these faces are as poignant as the face of their beautiful, threatened land.

Lou Rose is Associate Editor for Southern Maryland of the *Maryland Historical Magazine.*

WESTERN MARYLAND

While many Marylanders identify themselves by the county or city in which they live, the people of the western part of the state associate themselves with a region, an area characterized by mountains and valleys. When they see the outline of the Appalachian chain that juts across Washington County while driving home from another part of the state they experience an emotional divide: ahead is a congenial environment, behind them is disharmony. Flanked by mountains in the Hagerstown area and surrounded by them in Allegany and Garrett counties to the West, the people who live in this region are affected subliminally by the terrain. Those who work and play west of Sideling Hill, where the man-made cut was recently etched to accommodate Interstate Route 48, feel almost emotionally separated from the rest of the state. This sense of remoteness has historically shaped the character of a region popularly known as Western Maryland.

This symbolic separateness has nurtured independence in these people and pride in what they believe they have accomplished on their own. While the state government has provided more assistance to the region than its inhabitants concede, Western Marylanders take pride in having shaped their own lives. Whenever the chance is available to extract material wealth from the land or to manufacture and repair by machine or hand a useful product, they have succeeded. It is not uncommon for industrial workers to "moonlight" in specialized jobs and to return periodically to the site of their labor to inspect their finished work.

In his mini-classic nineteenth-century autobiography, *Forty-Four Years of the Life of a Hunter*, Meschach Browning dramatically recounts living off the land with his wife Mary near what is now Deep Creek Lake. Their self-sufficiency and mutual interdependence would typify later coal mining families in the George's Creek Valley of Allegany County. These qualities were also exhibited by road, canal and railroad builders and operators throughout the region. They are still true of modern industrial and service workers who now constitute the bulk of the area's working population. Men are easily replaced by women in leadership roles, as illustrated by Beverly Byron's appointment to the Congressional seat upon her husband's death and her virtually uncontested elections since.

Despite the many notable accomplishments of Western Marylanders, a certain defensiveness about themselves and their place has been a cultural by-product of the region's separateness. Historically affected by earlier frontier wars and adversity, then more profoundly from long periods of neglect from the state political capital, the people are often at odds with others. They are therefore quick to defend themselves, especially against outsiders' perception of them as rubes. Western Maryland, characterized by small towns and even smaller communities, lacks symphony orchestras, operas and art museums. Yet, a significant portion of its people spend many hours driving to Baltimore or Pittsburgh for concerts, theatrical plays and professional sporting events. Because their work or recreation take a growing number of Western Marylanders "downstate," or across it, many of them know more about the whole of Maryland than those who live in the state's cultural and economic hubs. For those who stay at home, community theatres, school-related athletic contests and central shopping malls provide enjoyment.

Western Marylanders also put a high premium on education for its own sake and as a way to achieve success. Historically, the literacy rate has been high. A coal miner, David J. Lewis, who later became a lawyer, state legislator and congressman, read Shakespeare on his breaks in the mines in the late nineteenth century. Another miner turned state legislator, John Leake, pioneered the creation of the state's second normal school in Frostburg in 1898. Ivy League college graduates from the region are fairly common.

More common are churches and their members whose social lives often revolve around institutionalized religion. The bitter inter-denominational conflict of the previous century, driven largely by ethnic solidarity, has given way to mutual respect and cooperative ventures. Organized church activities for fund-raising purposes to help people in need, repair steeples or support evangelical missions reflect a generous voluntaristic instinct. Religious fundamentalism, exemplified in a great number of revival meetings and a characteristically traditional theological outlook of the people, is still strong. So is the tendency of Catholics, almost as numerous as Protestants, to keep their parochial schools. A small black population maintains its own churches as do an equally small number of Jews sustain their congregations.

Western Marylanders are most pleased with their daily rhythm of life. Many of them drive to work in a few minutes. House doors are commonly left unlocked. They use first names and there are few secrets. They welcome outsiders into their homes. They are hospitable people who seek friendliness and conviviality in others.

Because of their natural pride, defensiveness and strong attachment to a particular place and way of life, Western Marylanders have also resisted change. Their character, marked by tested values and goals, is a conservative one, reluctant to experiment with cultural innovation. Their inwardness and individualism, shaped by their history and environment, also sometimes compound a reluctance to work together for a common regional good. Extensive distances between towns and parts of the area further preclude cooperative action. Separated geographically from each other often propelled by that ultimate ethnocentrism—the immediate and often far reaching extended family—Western Marylanders have sometimes been their own worst enemies. Communities have generally resisted united regional programs.

But their attachment to their local place, characterized by a relaxed way of life, is unyielding. The Monocacy Valley, the Catoctin Mountains, Sideling Hill, the Savage River and Deep Creek Lake, once the home of hunters, cattlemen, farmers, road builders and skilled craftspeople, still keep and lure people who want to extract something, now more psychological than material, from the land.

John B. Wiseman is Professor of History at Frostburg State University.

Above: *The setting sun illuminates a colorful Seneca tribesman at the AIITCO (American Indian Inter-Tribal Cultural Organization) Pow Wow in Garrett County. Tribes from all over the country participate in this annual gathering near McHenry, where the public is welcome to share in the traditions of native Americans.*

Left: *A red-tailed hawk keeps a watchful eye for rabbits and other rodents. Our most common bird of prey, this species can be found in almost every patch of woods throughout the state.*

Above: Sherwood Gardens in Baltimore explodes in color from late April to early May. Primarily a tulip garden, some 80,000 bulbs from Holland are planted each year. Also featured on the grounds are dogwood, azaleas, and magnolias.

Left: Winter paints farmland in a fresh coat of white. There are roughly 17,000 farms in the state, covering almost one half of the total land area.

Following Pages: Watermen converge on a newly opened oyster bed near Cambridge. As many as fifty boats of eager hand-tongers claim their spots before dawn breaks; the harvest commences at sunup. Oystering takes place during the "R" months, from September to April.

Above: *Members of the "Spray" family dig up autumn vegetables at the Godiah Spray Tobacco Plantation, an exhibit in Historic St. Mary's City. The working plantation, which depicts life in the 1660s, is one of several exhibits that recreates life at seventeenth-century "St. Maries Citty," the first permanent English settlement in Maryland, along the banks of the Potomac in St. Mary's County. Other highlights include the reconstructed state house of 1676, archaeology sites, and the Maryland Dove, an authentic working reconstruction of one of the two ships (the Ark and the Dove) which brought Maryland's first settlers on March 25, 1634.*

Left: *Pikemen of the St. Maries Citty Militia drill on the Governor's Field during the Maryland Days festival which celebrates the founding of the colony. The company of pikemen and musketeers, which recreates with great authenticity a fighting unit of the early 1600s, is distinguished as the "State's Official Seventeenth Century Troops."*

Right: *Rebecca Spray and child await the "Harvest Home" feast of the plantation, celebrating survival on the rugged frontier.*

Above: *Hounds anxiously await a foxhunt, or foxchase (the term preferred by some followers of the sport) at a country home near Monkton. The excitement of a hunt derives from chasing the clever fox, which usually outsmarts the pack of hounds; on rare occasions a sick or old fox is actually killed. The tradition has strong roots in Maryland, where America's first recorded foxhunt (1650) was conducted by an uprooted Englishman. There are currently sixteen organized foxhunting clubs in Maryland.*

Left: *Feed corn for livestock catches the last light of a November sunset; corn is second only to soybeans as Maryland's leading cash crop. Also known for its sweet corn, Maryland is home to several of the largest sweet corn canneries in the eastern United States.*

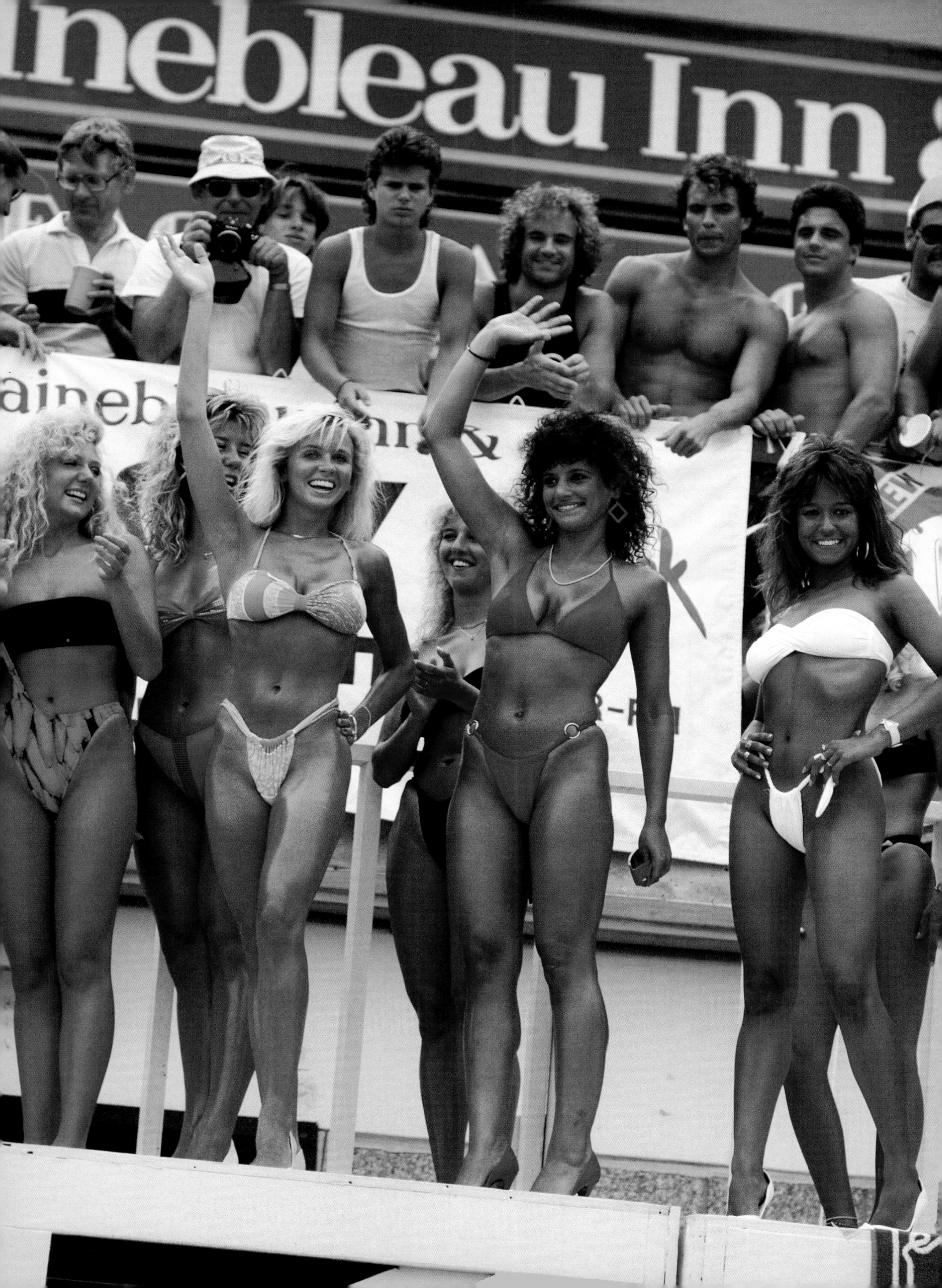
nebleau Inn

Above: *A waterskier passes a marker during the Deep Creek Lake Slalom Tournament at Paradise Point Cove. The lake is Maryland's largest, with a length of twelve miles and a total shoreline of sixty-five miles. In 1924 Deep Creek Lake was created by an electrical company, and it now serves as the heart of Garrett County's vacationland, offering swimming, boating, year-round fishing, skating, and snowmobiling.*

Left: *The three winners of a mid-summer Best Body on the Beach Contest offer their appreciation to a crowd of 5,000 spectators at the Sheraton Fontainbleu in Ocean City. The competitions are held each Sunday from Memorial Day to Labor Day, when winners return for the final contest to determine the best male and female bodies.*

Above: *Decorated in traditional Christmas lights in Baltimore's Inner Harbor, the U.S. Frigate Constellation is the first commissioned ship of the United States Navy. Launched from Fells Point in 1797, she is also the world's oldest continuously afloat warship.*

Left: *Inside the China Sea Marine Trading Company, the mood suits the goods: unusual and exotic marine salvage from around the world. Several items date back to the sixteenth century. Located in Baltimore's Fells Point, the store also serves as a ships chandler.*

Above: Within an hour of checking into the U.S. Naval Academy several plebes learn one of their first lessons: "dixie cup" hats are to fit "three fingers above the bridge of the nose." This class of 1,320 plebes comes from all fifty states and nine foreign countries. Some 6% will not make it through the grueling plebe summer.

Right: The fifteen Navy barbers have about four hours to cut all 1,320 heads. Men are trimmed to a hair length of an eighth of an inch, while women's hair can extend to the top of the neck.

Left: Tecumseh, also known as the "god of c" (the passing grade for midshipmen) is decked out in a fresh coat of war paint before special occasions like the Army-Navy football game. Pennies are frequently tossed in his quiver for good luck.

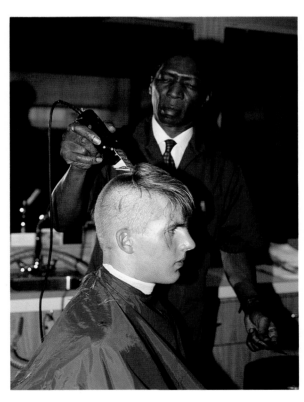

Above: *Crew members ride the springboards of a log canoe during a weekend race out of St. Michael's. Unique to the bay, there are perhaps twenty of these sleek sailboats left. The log canoe once numbered 1,600 in the mid-1800s, when it was the main workboat of watermen catching crabs and oysters. The hulls are made from three or five logs, an adaptation of the true log canoes of the Indians of the bay region, who carved their boats out of single logs. Organized sailing regattas for these tall-masted (and easily capsized) craft go back to 1859.*

Right: *The competition is stiff at the prestigious Fall Racing Series out of Annapolis, the last big event of the racing season.*

Left: *The Annapolis harbor is nearly overwhelmed during the annual U.S. Sailboat Show, held there since 1970. Visitors and exhibitors from all over the globe participate in this largest show of its kind in the world. The massive wooden dome of the State House looms in the distance. Maryland's State House briefly served as the capital of the United States from November 1783 to June 1784, and it has the distinction of being the nation's oldest capitol building in continuous legislative use.*

Above: *The quiet town of New Market has accommodated travelers since its founding in the late eighteenth century. Located in Frederick County along the National Pike, which extended from Baltimore to Cumberland, New Market was a popular resting place for settlers heading for the frontier.*

Right: *A container ship edges past Chesapeake City along the Chesapeake and Delaware Canal, which links the Chesapeake Bay with the Atlantic Ocean via the Delaware River. Opened for navigation in 1829, the route serves as a major shortcut to Baltimore for pleasure craft and ships from northern ports. Chesapeake City developed as a service stop for canal traffic, and it is home to the Old Lock Pump House (an exhibit of the Chesapeake and Delaware Canal Museum), which was once vital when the canal used locks.*

Following pages: *Skipjacks line the docks of Sandy Point State Park during Chesapeake Appreciation Days. First held in 1965, this maritime festival celebrates the skipjack, Maryland's official state boat. Fewer than thirty remain today, constituting America's last sail-powered commercial fleet.*

Above: *A jouster aims her lance during the Oxon Hill Jousting Tournament in Prince George's County. This ancient equestrian sport was introduced in Maryland by Cecil Calvert, the first Lord Baltimore, upon the founding of St. Mary's City in 1634, and it has thrived here since. In the Middle Ages knights would knock each other off their mounts, but today the sport involves spearing nine rings on three charges; rings as small as one-quarter of an inch in diameter are used. Jousting is the official state sport in Maryland, the only state to have an official sport.*

Left: *The University of Maryland Terrapins, a perennial power in lacrosse, discuss strategy during a game. An unsuccessful attempt has been made to have lacrosse declared as Maryland's official state sport.*

Above: *A favorite attraction along the boardwalk in Ocean City is Flashback Old Time Photos, where one can be transformed within minutes into a variety of characters, ranging from pirates to gangsters. The most popular characters are cowboys and barmaids.*

Right: *Counselors play a game of cowboy polo during a rodeo at the River Valley Ranch, located near Millers in Carroll County. In 1953 the ranch was established by two Baltimore ministers to serve as a summer camp where young people could be introduced to the message of God. A Christian atmosphere blends in with the western setting where campers from the mid-Atlantic area enjoy trail riding, swimming, hay rides, archery, and a rodeo, which concludes each week-long session.*

Above: *Row houses and sparkling white marble steps are distinguishing features of Baltimore's urban landscape. Some of their more famous residents include Babe Ruth, Edgar Allan Poe, H. L. Mencken, and Governor William Donald Schaefer.*

Left: *Christmas lights adorn the Washington Monument in Baltimore's elegant Mount Vernon Place. This 108-foot memorial is the first monument begun (1815) in honor of George Washington. Baltimore has been nicknamed the "Monumental City" for its wealth of statues and monuments.*

Above: *Watermen haul in their fyke nets along the Chester River in Kent County. Perhaps a dozen such rigs in the upper bay are still used to catch white perch, yellow perch, catfish, carp, and a few other kinds of fish. The idea for the trap was first developed by local Indians who fished the Chesapeake Bay centuries ago.*

Left: *A tobacco farmer of countless generations proudly displays a "stick" of tobacco leaves before hanging it to dry in his Charles County barn. Harvested in August, the tobacco will cure in the vented barn through winter, when the leaves will then be stripped from the stalk and prepared for market. Once the predominant crop of colonial days, tobacco is still grown in five Maryland counties.*

Above: Thoroughbreds get off to a close start at Pimlico Race Course in Baltimore. Pimlico is operated by the Maryland Jockey Club, formed in 1743, making it the oldest sporting organization in America. Racing at Pimlico commenced in 1870, and an average of 1.3 million dollars are bet daily during a typical season of racing. Pimlico is also home to the National Jockeys Hall of Fame.

Right: Just ten hours old, a bashful foal tests his legs in the warmth of a springtime sun. Maryland's green pastures have nourished countless champions of the racing world.

Following Pages: Dusk sets in over "Charm City." With a population of 786,775 in 1980, Baltimore is the twelfth largest city in the United States.

Above and left: *Classic Maryland farmland maintains a timeless quality. The fertile Piedmont region, which extends from New Jersey to Alabama, runs through central Maryland, supporting a wide range of crops. The area is also the heart of Maryland's dairy farming industry.*

Right: *A sheep farmer takes a break from the competitions at the Maryland Sheep and Wool Festival in Howard County.*

es of parades each year bring color and
ement to streets throughout Maryland. Some of
arger parades include the Autumn Glory
de in Oakland (Queen with flowers), the
kness Parade in Baltimore (boy and girl), the
rate Carroll County Anniversary (150th)
de in Westminster (clowns, covered wagon and
float), the I Am An American Day Parade in
more (Mummers and the Noid), and the
ication Procession in Baltimore (couples in
ial garb).

Above: Competitors embark on a rugged 8K cross-country ski race at Herrington Manor State Park in Garrett County, Maryland's mountain playground. Known as the "Switzerland of America," the county offers a tremendous range of outdoor adventures. Residents are especially proud of the powerful Savage River, site of the 1989 Whitewater World Championships, involving over 200 athletes from at least twenty countries. In two decades of world whitewater events, the 1989 competition is the first held in American waters.

Right: Kayakers take a break from the strong currents of the Potomac River at Great Falls of the Potomac, located ten miles above Washington, D.C., in Montgomery County. The river drops seventy-seven feet in three-quarters of a mile, creating challenging whitewater. Expert kayakers occasionally go down the falls. Though the Potomac forms a border between Maryland and Virginia, the river belongs to Maryland.

No beach vacation is complete without riding the Ferris wheel **(above)**, *flying kites* **(right)**, *feeding the friendly seagulls* **(left)**, *and dodging boardwalk trains* **(above left)**. *Ocean City is situated on a vulnerable ten-mile long Atlantic barrier island which is only a quarter-mile wide. In 1933 a powerful storm cut out the inlet which now separates Ocean City from Assateague Island; this disaster was actually a blessing, for it provided ocean access to Sinepuxent Bay, where fishing and pleasure boats can enjoy protected anchorage.*

Above: *An Amish boy sprints home from his one-room schoolhouse. In 1939 several Pennsylvania Amish families packed their bags and settled near Charlotte Hall, a small town in northern St. Mary's County. The present community of 250 families is respected for their farming and business skills. Modern conveniences like electricity, the automobile, and tractors are rejected. Instead, windmills pump water on their farms and horses pull buggies and plows. The county is also home to a community of 110 Mennonite families.*

Right: *Runners fill Light Street during the annual Constellation 10K run through the streets of Baltimore. Some 3,400 competitors turned out for this race in 1987.*

Above: *An exuberant retriever faithfully fetches a Canada goose, shot down along the Chester River. Duck and goose hunting is big business on the Eastern Shore, attracting over 60,000 hunters each winter from all over the country. The Chesapeake Bay offers the best waterfowl hunting along the Atlantic Flyway, a complex network of migration routes extending from Canada to the Gulf of Mexico.*

Left: *A ring-necked pheasant keeps a watchful eye in a Kent County cornfield. These prized game birds were introduced from the Orient in the late nineteenth century, much to the delight of nature-lovers and hunters. They are found in woods and fields across the state, but pheasants on the Eastern Shore are seen only near one of the several game preserves, where they are released for hunting.*

Above: *Sentimental Journey Antiques offers holiday cheer along Talbot Street in historic St. Michaels. Home to the Chesapeake Bay Maritime Museum, this quaint Talbot County town takes great pride as "the town that fooled the British." During the War of 1812, the British planned to burn this important shipbuilding center, but residents hung lanterns beyond the town limits, thus fooling the British gunners into overshooting their target.*

Left: *Our Lady Star of the Sea marks the entrance to Solomons, located at the southern tip of Calvert County. This community thrived on its seafood processing industry and shipbuilding earlier in the century; today Solomons maintains a slower pace. Yet this quiet fishing village is becoming increasingly popular for its deep sheltered harbor (regarded as one the finest on the East Coast), attracting thousands of yachtsmen each summer.*

Offering something for everyone, the Maryland State Fair has been going strong since 1878; nearly half a million loyal Marylanders pass through the gates each year. About 15,000 ribbons are awarded annually in the categories of 4H, home arts, livestock and farm and garden.

Above: The Tagart Memorial Chapel marks the campus of McDonogh School near Owings Mills. Freedom of religion has strong roots in Maryland. In 1649 the right to worship according to one's own belief was first protected by law at St. Mary's City; this act was the first in colonial America to separate church and state.

Right: At Atlanta Hall Farm a thoroughbred is escorted to the starting line of a timber race during the Elkridge-Harford Point-to-Point. For more than fifty years this series of timber races has served as a preparation for Maryland's Triple Crown of steeplechasing—My Lady's Manor, the Grand National, and the Maryland Hunt Cup.

Following pages: Cumberland endures a long, harsh winter in the Allegheny Mountains. Situated along the Potomac River amidst several mountains rising at least 1,000 feet, the city was originally a frontier trading post in the mid-1700s.

Above: The isolated town of Tylerton on Smith Island clings stubbornly to a threatened way of life. Smith Island is actually a series of islands in the Chesapeake Bay located twelve miles off Crisfield. The 750 residents of the three towns—Ewell, Rhodes Point, and Tylerton—have always derived their living from the water. They are descendents of the original English settlers who arrived here from Cornwall in 1657. Isolation has preserved the distinct Cornish accent of these rugged individuals, who rely on nicknames, as most of the islanders have the surname Evans, Bradshaw, or Tyler.

Left: A warm spring afternoon makes a hard day's work a bit more enjoyable for this waterman from Cambridge.

Right: Time takes its toll on a once well-traveled boardwalk to a waterman's shanty on Smith Island. The island is quite vulnerable to the current high rate of erosion. Every year the Smith Island cluster becomes smaller and smaller; some residents can remember islands which have long since been reclaimed by the Chesapeake Bay.

Above: *The Maryland Heights cliffs, near the town of Sandy Hook, offer an impressive view of Harpers Ferry, West Virginia, located at the intersection of the Potomac and Shenandoah Rivers.*

Left: *A strong side-shore wind lures Ocean City's expert windsurfers from the less challenging waters of Assawoman Bay to the Atlantic surf. Occasionally the wind dies suddenly, leaving windsurfers with a long paddle back to shore.*

Following pages: *The Elkridge-Harford Hunt enjoys Maryland's spectacular countryside during the Thanksgiving Day hunt near Monkton. The day commences with the traditional Blessing of the Hounds at St. James Church; this old English ceremony has been going strong in Maryland since colonial days.*

Above: *A Baltimore City fireboat joins in the celebration of National Flag Day USA.*

Right: *The Milk-Off competition at the Harborplace Amphitheatre highlights Harvest on the Harbor.*

Left: *Santa's Place offers promises of a bountiful Christmas for toddlers at the Inner Harbor.*

Above: *A sheep farmer awaits the judge's decision during a competition at the Maryland Sheep and Wool Festival in Howard County. This annual show, the largest of its kind in the country, draws scores of sheep farmers from all over Maryland and from many states east of the Mississippi. Besides sheep judgings (over twenty breeds of sheep are on display), the festival puts on shearing competitions, working sheep dog demonstrations, the Maryland Wool Queen competition, auctions, and related foods and crafts displays.*

Left: *Summer heat takes its toll at the Polish Festival in Baltimore. The city cherishes its ethnic diversity, celebrated during the summer-long "Showcase of Nations," featuring fourteen ethnic groups. Since the early 1900s Baltimore's ethnic communities have shared with the public their music, dance, costumes, food, crafts, and religion.*

Above: In Ocean City, one of the boardwalk's unexpected attractions are huge sand sculptures, created all summer long by one individual in an attempt to spread the message of Jesus. Hours of meticulous work go into each piece as large crowds form in appreciation of this unusual art form.

Left: Beach goers enjoy the two and one-half mile long boardwalk on a warm August evening. The population of Ocean City swells from nearly 8,000 permanent residents to 300,000 during peak summer weekends, attracting vacationers from all over the mid-Atlantic area.

Above: *Whitewater enthusiasts from Precision Rafting negotiate one of the Youghiogheny's twenty class 4 or 5 rapids; the highest rating is class 6, considered to be life-threatening, even to experts. Since 1981, rafting on this ten-mile run in western Garrett County has grown in popularity; there are currently about ten companies working the river. With an average drop of 116 feet per mile, the run is acknowledged as the steepest and most technically demanding stretch of whitewater east of the Mississippi.*

Right: *Maryland's woods offer a variety of hiking trails, including a portion of the famed Appalachian Trail, which runs for thirty-eight miles between Frederick and Washington Counties. Extending over 2,100 miles from Maine to Georgia, the Appalachian Trail crosses fourteen states. Each year more than 100 hearty souls hike the entire distance over a period of four to six months.*

Maryland is home to a diverse collection of water birds, including (counterclockwise) the great blue heron, mallard ducks, osprey, Canada geese (also pictured below), the wood duck, and the bald eagle. Our national symbol has made a gradual comeback in the Chesapeake Bay area; about ninety pairs currently nest in Maryland, representing the fifth largest nesting area of bald eagles in the nation.

89

Above: *One of Baltimore's famed "Ay-rabs" proudly displays some of the city's finest produce. These urban nomads have roamed the streets of Baltimore for as long as anyone can remember, peddling fruit, vegetables and other treats from their wagons.*

Left: *After a hard day's work, a father and son display a portion of their catch: the delicious Maryland blue crab. Young watermen are a dying breed, but this youngster has spent his summers working alongside his father since the age of four. Currently there are some 5,000 watermen who earn a living harvesting the riches of the Chesapeake Bay. It is difficult work (a typical workday starts several hours before sunrise), and recent ecological problems of the bay have made it a less attractive occupation, but the force of tradition carries this vulnerable way of life.*

Following pages: *Hot-air balloons prepare to lift off from Druid Hill Park in Baltimore during the Preakness Balloon Race to the Eastern Shore. This colorful event is one of many that leads up to the Preakness Stakes at Pimlico Race Course.*

Above: *Hampton Mansion, the focal point of Hampton National Historic Site near Towson in Baltimore County, is generally regarded as one of the most impressive post-Revolutionary War mansions in America. Built between 1783 and 1790 in the late Georgian style, the mansion was home to the Ridgely family for 158 years, before being turned over to the National Park Service in 1948.*

Left: *The flag is lowered after a full day of activities during the Military Field Days event at Fort Frederick State Park in Washington County. Held each June, the program involves nearly 400 men and women, each meticulously dressed in historical attire, who reenact camp scenes and engage in tactical battlefield maneuvers from the French and Indian, Revolutionary, and Civil Wars. The fort was built in 1756 as a cornerstone of British defense against the French, who were also vying for imperial control of North America. It has the distinction of being the only remaining original French and Indian War fort in America.*

Above: *The Double Dip has faithfully served the town of Denton since 1922. Several daily customers have patronized this Caroline County establishment for more than a decade, swapping stories while enjoying the delicious twenty-four flavors of home-made ice cream.*

Left: *The storekeeper enjoys a game of checkers with his daughter at R. H. Wilson & Son General Merchandising, located west of Hagerstown near the town of Wilson. The store was built in 1852 to accommodate travelers along the National Pike, gateway to the West. Believed to be the oldest general store in Maryland, R. H. Wilson & Son was restored in 1984 to its old-time look, after being closed for a decade. Not surprisingly, it has become a tourist attraction.*

Above: *The Victorian facade of Johns Hopkins Hospital is a familiar sight to the international medical community. The hospital opened in 1889 and it has since earned a worldwide reputation for excellence in patient care, medical education and research.*

Right: *Sailors enjoy a dramatic view of the National Aquarium's striking geometry. Since its opening in 1981, the Aquarium has become Baltimore's most popular tourist attraction. More than 5,000 specimens of fish, amphibians, reptiles, mammals, and birds (representing 600 species) are presented in a variety of habitats, including an Atlantic coral reef, a tropical rain forest, and an ocean tank filled with sharks and other ocean fish. Two favorite exhibits are a pair of Beluga whales and an outdoor seal pool.*

Following pages: *Maryland waters offer some of the finest sailing in the country. (**clockwise from top**) Spinnakers fly during the start of a Wednesday night race out of Annapolis. The Lady Maryland schooner is dwarfed by a passing container ship. Ocean City vacationers embark on a catamaran cruise on Assawoman Bay. Shipjacks race off of Sandy Point State Park during Chesapeake Appreciation Days.*

Above: *Steeplechase fans take delight in tailgating parties before the running of the Hunt Cup in Worthington Valley. First run in 1894, this race (the oldest steeplechase still running in the country) is considered the toughest timber race in the world, covering a four mile course of twenty-two timber fences. The top three finishers are invited to compete in the equally demanding Grand National Steeplechase (over brush fences) in England.*

Left: *The Baltimore Symphony Orchestra delights a large crowd at Oregon Ridge Park during the Summer Concert Series. Under the direction of David Zinman, the world class orchestra completed a tour of Europe and the Soviet Union in the summer of 1987, making it the first American symphony to perform in Moscow in a decade. The Meyerhoff Symphony Hall in Baltimore, one of the most modern concert halls in the world, is the permanent home of the orchestra.*

Following pages: *Charles Fenwick, Jr., (in orange and green) edges past John B. Hannum, Jr., on the way to his fifth Maryland Hunt Cup victory in 1987. Fenwick, who holds the course record of 8.33-⅗ minutes (made by Ben Nevis II in 1978) has also won the Grand National Steeplechase in England.*

Moments of natural splendor abound to the discerning eye. An early morning frost (**above left**) heralds the arrival of autumn. Day lilies (**above right**) dot the mid-summer landscape of Maryland in bright orange. Barley (**below**) wilts during a particularly dry summer. Glazed winter berries (**right**) fall victim to an ice storm.

Following Pages: Morning mist settles near Bosley United Methodist Church in the countryside of Baltimore County.

Above: *A first-place blue marlin is proudly displayed at Harbour Island Marina during the annual White Marlin Open in Ocean City, which calls itself "White Marlin Capital of the World." First held in 1974, this contest has become the largest billfish tournament on the East Coast, drawing nearly 200 boatloads of hopeful anglers in 1987. The official purse of $45,000 (and a rumored $300,000 in unofficial wagering) is divided among the categories of white marlin, blue marlin, tuna, wahoo, dolphin and shark.*

Left: *When ordering fresh Maine lobster in Ocean City restaurants, chances are that your dinner was actually caught about sixty miles off Ocean City. Maryland's fledgling lobster fleet (only twenty years old) consists of four boats, with just one boat fishing exclusively for lobsters. Traps are laid along the continental shelf at a depth of 50 to 150 fathoms.*

Above: Boordy Vineyards offers a glimpse of rural France in Baltimore County. Founded in 1945, Boordy is Maryland's oldest and largest winery, producing over 100,000 bottles each year. Among their twelve red, white, and blush wines are award winners at competitions for eastern United States and Canada vineyards. There are currently thirteen wineries in the Association of Maryland Wineries.

Right: New Market is a delight to antique collectors. With more than forty shops from which to choose, the town has earned the nickname "Antiques Capital of Maryland."

Marylanders take great pride in their history, evidenced by the wealth of related events. The garb of a French fur trapper (**left**) at Fort Frederick State Park indicates his association with Indians during the French and Indian War. A wedding attendant (**above left**) awaits the procession during a Victorian wedding at the Surratt House in Clinton; the house was home to Mary Surratt, who was hanged for her alleged role in the assassination of President Lincoln. Sisters (**above right**) of the Tone-Pah-Hote family, representing the Kiowa tribe of Oklahoma, dance at the Brandywine Pow Wow. A Revolutionary War unit (**below**) attacks British forces during a battle at Fort Frederick State Park.

Above: *A tugboat assists in the docking of a container ship. Annually the port of Baltimore serves some 3,000 ships representing nearly every seagoing nation of the world. As the sixth largest port in the country, Baltimore's terminals can handle 200 ships simultaneously at full capacity.*

Left: *The Lady Maryland offers schoolchildren throughout the state a unique opportunity to learn about the Chesapeake Bay, its history, ecology, sailing, economics and geography. Launched from the Inner Harbor in June 1986, she is a full size replica of the Pungy schooner. These sleek workboats graced the bay during the 1800s, transporting perishable cargo and luxury items. Hands-on education is stressed aboard the Lady Maryland. Included in a day's activities are raising the sails, conducting ecological tests, tying knots, and swabbing the decks.*

Above: *Joyous sorority sisters celebrate the arrival of another weekend at Washington College in Chestertown. Established in 1782, it is the first American college named in honor of George Washington, as well as Maryland's first chartered college. Maryland has more than seventy colleges and universities.*

Right: *Midshipmen of the Naval Academy drill on Worden Field during the Dedication Parade of Commissioning Week. This week-long celebration in May (which culminates in graduation) includes dances and balls, concerts, sailboat processions, and Blue Angels flight demonstrations.*

Following pages: *An Amish tobacco farmer awaits his turn to unload his prized crop at the Hughesville warehouse in Charles County. The rugged horses pull the wagon for several miles along the main highway as automobiles speed by.*

Above: *A window washer insures a clear view of the Inner Harbor for guests of the Hyatt Regency Baltimore. As recently as the mid-1960s the waterfront was in a state of decay, but the Inner Harbor was targeted for the revitalization of downtown Baltimore, and it has since flourished.*

Right: *Rush-hour traffic inundates Charles Street in Baltimore.*

Summer fun in Maryland takes a variety of forms. Bull riding (**above and left**) is a favorite rodeo event at the River Valley Ranch. Along with ten bulls, the ranch is home to eight buffalo and dozens of horses. The public is welcome to attend the rodeo and stroll through the western town of twenty buildings, including the Wells Fargo Stage Depot, the Doc's Office, the Wrangler's Roost, and the Long Horn Lodge. A youngster (**above left**) celebrates summertime at Beaver Dam Swim Club. Marylanders have been escaping summer heat in the cool waters of the Beaver Dam quarry for more than fifty years. Whitewater enthusiasts (**right**) enjoy "surfing" one of the Youghiogheny's powerful rapids; the maneuver involves paddling into a rapid and battling the backcurrent at the base of the falls.

Above: *A pair of great horned owls appear undaunted by a winter storm. The largest of Maryland's seven species of owls, adult great horned owls are seen together only during the mating season; otherwise they lead solitary lives.*

Left: *Hikers in Cunningham Falls State Park enjoy the view above the sixty-eight foot cascading waterfalls for which the park is named. Other recreational activities offered by the park are camping, hunting, canoeing, swimming, cross-country skiing, and riding.*

Above: *Like generations before him, the owner of Mulberry Fields whiles away a spring afternoon on the riverfront balcony. Built in 1755 along the Potomac River near Beauvue in St. Mary's County, Mulberry Fields is one of Maryland's grand plantation homes. In its heyday nearly 200 slaves worked the self-sufficient plantation village of 10,000 acres; main cash crops were tobacco, cotton, wheat, corn and flax. Today only a few crops are still cultivated with the help of two families, descendants of the slaves who once worked there.*

Right: *Cypress "knees" dot the landscape of Battle Creek Cypress Swamp, providing stability for the trees and oxygen to the submerged roots. Located in Calvert County, this 100-acre swamp is the northernmost naturally occurring cluster of bald cypress trees on the continent. Such swamps covered a large portion of Maryland in the days when mammoths and sabertoothed tigers roamed the land.*

Above: *A fiery maple tree keeps company with an old barn in the mountains of Western Maryland. All of Garrett County lies within the Appalachian Plateau, and several of its larger mountains form a section of the eastern continental divide.*

Left: *Once a valuable assistant to the orchard keeper, an old wagon falls victim to the elements. There are approximately 500 orchards in Maryland; the largest are concentrated along the Appalachian apple belt near Hancock in Washington County.*

Above: *Fresh from the bay, these blue crabs will end up on someone's dinner table within a matter of hours. This crustacean does not look very intelligent, but watermen attribute to them legendary cunning, and an extensive vocabulary has developed to describe their unique traits and behaviors. Maryland watermen catch nearly 50 million pounds of blue crabs each year in the Chesapeake Bay, and that, coupled with the Virginia catch, accounts for half of the nation's blue crab harvest.*

Right: *The Atlantic Ocean and the Chesapeake Bay provide a vast array of culinary delights.* **(clockwise from top)** *A large carp is unloaded from a pound net in the Chester River; this technique of trapping fish was first developed by the Indian tribes who lived there. Soft-shell clams are picked off of a conveyor-belt rig which extends to the shallow bottom near Rock Hall. Oysters are brought to the surface of the Choptank River with eighteen-foot-long tongs. Lobsters are banded soon after being trapped sixty miles out into the Atlantic.*

Above: *Flowers are plentiful at Baltimore's annual Flower Mart, a ritual of spring since 1911. The Women's Civic League and local garden clubs sell flowers with a smile from booths and tables which encircle the Washington Monument in historic Mount Vernon Place. The celebration, held in early May, offers crafts, entertainment, food, and the ever-popular lemon with an embedded stick of peppermint.*

Left: *Students of the Johns Hopkins University chat in front of Gilman Hall, the central building on the campus. Founded in 1876, the University was the vision of Johns Hopkins, a successful Maryland merchant who set aside $7,000,000 for the establishment of a university and hospital. Arguably the first true university in America, Johns Hopkins University is also home to the Lacrosse Hall of Fame.*

Happy faces abound at Maryland events. (clockwise from top): Suntanned contestants await the judges' choice of Miss Ocean City 1987. The Leprechaun Look-Alike Contest highlights the St. Patrick's Day celebration at Baltimore's War Memorial Plaza. Winners of the Best Body on the Beach Contest (1987) pose. Bill the Goat poses with cheerleaders of the U.S. Naval Academy before the big game with Army. Spuds pays a surprise visit to the Governor's crab feast in Chestertown. Miss and Mr. Ocean City 1987 celebrate their victory. The Wschodnia Galicja Polish Folk Theatre performs at Baltimore's Polish Festival.

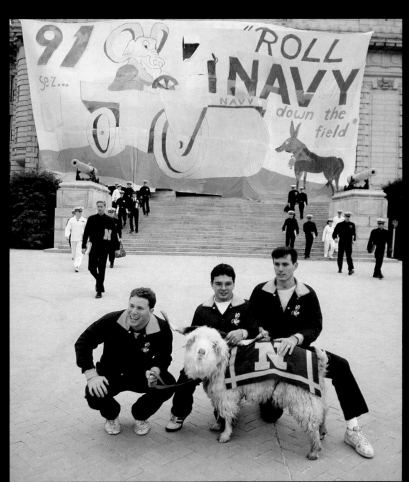

Above: *A familiar attraction of Fells Point is the China Sea Marine Trading Company, whose facade is a strong reminder of the days when drunken sailors stumbled from the pubs back to their tall ships, docked along the misty piers. The entire waterfront area, complete with its original Belgian block paving, retains an old-time look and has served as a location for old sailing movies.*

Right: *Owner Stevens Bunker enjoys the company of Singapore and Saigon, two of the store's noisy residents.*

Following pages: *The Libertad of Argentina makes a royal departure from Baltimore's Inner Harbor. Through the efforts of Operation Sail, over half of the world's majestic Tall Ships have visited Maryland in the past decade.*

Above: *Irate colonists storm a British ship during the annual Chestertown Tea Party. This reenactment is the highlight of the two-day celebration, which honors the Chestertown Tea Party of May 23, 1774, when Chestertonians cast chests of tea from the British brigantine Geddes into the Chester River, protesting taxation without representation. Appparently, the fervor of the Boston Tea Party, just five months earlier, had an influence on this act of rebellion against the Mother Country.*

Left: *The Plebe Recognition Ceremony can be a messy affair. Held each spring during Commissioning Week at the U.S. Naval Academy, this annual ritual is the culmination of a year-long series of rigors inflicted on the plebes by the upperclassmen. The object is to recover a "dixie cup" hat, which rests on the top of the Herndon Monument, and replace it with a navy cap. A human pyramid must be formed to reach the top, but the task is made difficult by a thick coat of lard covering the entire monument. The instant that the feat is accomplished, plebe year is over. Over the years, elapsed time in reaching the top has ranged from three minutes to three hours.*

Above: *The bounty of Queen Anne's County signals passers-by that Halloween is just around the corner. In the summer and fall roadside produce stands abound on Maryland's Eastern Shore, the predominant agricultural region of the state. Major crops include soybeans, wheat, corn, tomatoes and watermelons.*

Right: *Dusk sets in over the harbor of Ewell on Smith Island, as the Island Belle (towards the right) is slowly reclaimed by the bay that she once traversed daily. Today the Island Bell II and one other ferry provide the same essential services of mail and food delivery, transportation to the mainland for school and shopping, and delivery of tasty soft-shell crabs to local distributors.*

Following Pages: *Thoroughbreds are a frequent element of the Baltimore County landscape. With over 130 horse farms, this county offers more breeding and training facilities than any other in Maryland.*

147

Above: *A kayaker fights the powerful whitewater at Great Falls of the Potomac. On peak days as many as twenty kayakers congregate on this famous spot along the Potomac River.*

Right: *Windsurfers await a breeze at Sandy Point State Park, located next to the Chesapeake Bay Bridge. The first span was completed in 1952 at a length of 4.3 miles; a parallel bridge was added in 1973 to accommodate the growing traffic pressures, which reach a height on summer weekends as vacationers flock to Ocean City.*

Left: *When the wind blows hard enough to close sailboard rentals, Ocean City's windsurfing buffs flock to Assawoman Bay to practice the latest moves.*

Above: *Wilbur Ross Hubbard, born in 1896, prepares for a foxhunt near his Chestertown home. Hubbard, who began foxhunting in 1908, acquired his first pack of hounds in 1931. Since then he has entertained foxhunters from all over the United States and the British Isles. His guests are made quite comfortable in Widehall, his colonial mansion built in 1769. Still an avid foxhunter, he is the world's oldest Master of Foxhounds.*

Left: *A falconer prepares for a hunt in the woods of Howard County; he will frighten rabbits out of their hiding places, and his red-tailed hawk will swoop down and grasp the prey with lethal talons. In Maryland there are currently ninety falconers who fly three kinds of hawks and the endangered peregrine falcon.*

Following pages: *The last rays of an October sunset strike a Hereford cow and her calf.*

Emotions run high in the fast-pace, often punishing game of lacrosse. Since the establishment of an NCAA national lacrosse tournament in 1971, Maryland teams have won the title nine times, including seven championships by the Johns Hopkins University Blue Jays. This oldest sport in North America dates back to the 1400s, when Indian tribes played the game to condition their braves for warfare and to settle tribal disputes. Teams were composed of hundreds of warriors, goals were often miles apart, and games lasted for two or three days at a time.

The Preakness, held each May at Pimlico Race Course, is the second jewel of thoroughbred racing's famed Triple Crown for the fastest three-year-olds in the nation. A jubilant Chris McCarron (**above**) sits atop Alysheba, winner of the 112th running of the Preakness and 1987 Kentucky Derby.

Immediately after the race a workman (**right**) paints the colors of the winner on the weather vane atop the cupola in the winners' circle, where they will remain until the following Preakness. The Preakness infield (**below**) is home to Maryland's biggest party; crowds as large as 87,000 persons attend the Preakness, and nearly six million dollars (on track) will change hands during this full day of racing. The Preakness Parade (**facing page**) is one of many celebrations leading up to the big race. Other activities include a hot-air balloon race, a frog hop, a Pee Wee Preakness for school children, concerts, and neighborhood festivals.

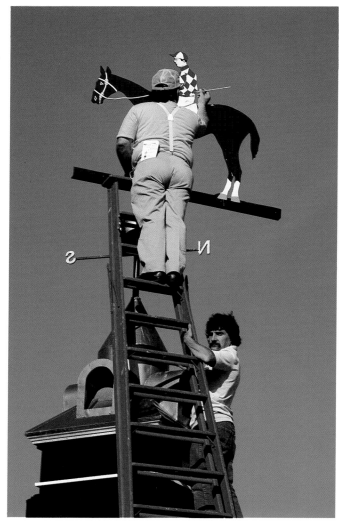

Above: *A resident of the small town of Accident prepares for a harsh Western Maryland winter. Garrett County receives nine times the average snowfall of the Eastern Shore. The town's name is derived from an incident in 1774, when the surrounding valley was mistakenly surveyed twice as the frontier was opened for settlement.*

Left: *Wisp Ski Area brims with action on a January weekend. Situated on Marsh Mountain (elevation 3,080 feet) next to Deep Creek Lake, Wisp is Maryland's largest ski area, offering twenty-three trails, from beginner to advanced, which cover nearly fifteen miles. The season runs from December to mid-March, concluding with the grand Winterfest celebration.*

Above: Variety in Motion takes juggling to the limits at the Harborplace Amphitheatre during the annual Street Performers Festival. *The seemingly countless attractions of the Inner Harbor draw millions of visitors each year.*

Left: *The waters of the Inner Harbor have lured nearly every type of boat from skiffs and paddle boats to tall ships and modern warships. The dome of City Hall rises in the distance.*

Above: *Frontier rifles, replicating those of the Revolutionary War period, are displayed outside the workshop of a Garrett County craftsman. Nearly 100 hours of meticulous labor are required to complete each unique rifle, which sells for an average of $450. Accuracy is excellent up to 100 yards.*

Left: *A trout fisherman tests his skills in Cunningham Falls State Park in Frederick County. Brook trout naturally thrive here, and the streams have been stocked with brown and rainbow trout, but all caught fish must be returned to the water. The park is set in the Catoctin Mountains, a branch of the Appalachian chain. A few miles away is Camp David, the presidential retreat first used by Franklin D. Roosevelt.*

Following page: *Ospreys, also known as "fish hawks," raise a new generation in their nest on the Chester River, after wintering in South America. Since the 1972 ban on DDT, ospreys have made a strong comeback in the Chesapeake Bay area, which now represents their largest single breeding population in North America. Living almost exclusively on a diet of fish, ospreys return to the same nest each year to raise an average clutch of two chicks.*

Above: *A classic American tradition is still going strong at the Dairy Queen in Odenton, located in Anne Arundel County. On Saturday nights from late spring to early fall antique car collectors from all over Maryland and neighboring states gather to display their cars. Up to sixty cars—some dating back to the 1920s—and hundreds of admirers pack the lot while popular tunes blare over the loudspeakers.*

Right: *The "good old days" are immortalized on the tailgate of a 1959 Chevrolet El Camino, which is frequently seen at the Dairy Queen.*

Left: *Anxious farmers stand by at the Hughesville warehouse while buyers respond to the rapid-fire chant of a tobacco auctioneer. Such auctions take place from mid-March to May at seven warehouses in Southern Maryland. Among the foreign buyers the Germans and Swiss especially like the Maryland leaf, which is regarded as more aromatic and faster burning than the tobacco of other states. In colonial Maryland, tobacco was king, often serving as currency in the fledgling economy.*

The Maryland Renaissance Festival, begun in 1977, has become one of Maryland's most popular events, drawing up to 109,000 visitors over its six-weekend duration. Since 1985 the festival has been set in a permanent Renaissance village near Crownsville in Anne Arundel County. Constant entertainment is provided by more than 600 performers, artisans, and Renaissance characters.

Above: *Pietro Francavilla's "The Apollo" (1591) highlights the Renaissance Sculpture Court of the renovated 1904 building at Baltimore's Walters Art Gallery. Regarded as one of America's finest comprehensive art museums, the gallery boasts a collection of 25,000 works, spanning 5,000 years of human creativity. The museum was originally built to house the private collection of Henry Walters, who bequeathed his collection, gallery, and house in 1931 to the city of Baltimore "for the benefit of the people."*

Left: *A Korean student of the cello practices at the Peabody Conservatory of Music in Baltimore. Talented musicians come from all over the world to receive instruction from a faculty of international recognition. Founded in 1857, the Peabody Institute was endowed by George Peabody, wealthy merchant and banker, who was dedicated to the cultural enrichment of Baltimore. The Peabody Library holds a rare music collection, including original manuscripts of Beethoven, Handel, and other famous composers.*

Despite a peak population density of 40,000 people per square mile, Ocean City still offers to vacationers moments of tranquility, including bicycle riding (**left**) in the morning, sandcastle-building (**above**), fishing (**above right**) from the bayside pier, and strolling (**right**) the boards near the Kite Loft, where each day there is an impressive display of unusual kites, wind permitting.

Above: *Freshly picked apples await a cider press at an orchard near Bel Air.*

Left: *At Brenneman's Grove in Garrett County sap has been gathered from ancient maple trees since the late 1800s. First practiced by the Indians, the art of maple sugaring takes place from late February to early April, when the combination of freezing night temperatures and warm days force the trees to leak. Once commonplace, maple sugaring is still practiced at nearly a dozen groves in Western Maryland.*

Right: *A lonely turkey welcomes visitors to the National Colonial Farm in Prince George's County. Situated along the banks of the Potomac, directly across from George Washington's Mount Vernon estate, this working farm recreates life during the time of the American Revolution, featuring such activities as planting, spinning, blacksmithing and candle making. The farm also hosts special historical reenactments each year.*

Above: The highlight of the St. Mary's County Oyster Festival is the National Oyster Shucking Contest, first held in 1969. Shuckers come from all over the Pacific, Gulf and Atlantic coasts to compete for the title of national champion, which is determined by a shuck-off between the men's and women's champion. Style and neatness are just as important as elapsed time. Men have won the title more often, but the only person ever to win three years in a row is a woman (Ruth Smith) from Maryland.

Right: A new national champion, Duke Landry (from Louisiana), is congratulated by the Oyster King. Landry represented the United States at the World Oyster Shucking Championship in Ireland.

Left: The Crab Picking Contest is one of the festivities of the National Hard Crab Derby in Crisfield. The origins of the Derby go back to 1947, when a few Crisfield men dropped a couple of live hard crabs in a circle on Main Street. The festival has grown to span the Labor Day weekend, featuring a parade, the Miss Crustacean Pageant, a boat docking contest, and the famous crab races. Crisfield is known as the "Seafood Capital of the World."

Above: *Wild ponies of Assateague Island rest on the dunes during the intense summer heat. This 35-mile-long Atlantic barrier island of sand dunes and salt marsh is shared with Virignia, which owns about one-third of the area. The smaller size of the distinctly-marked ponies is attributed mainly to a limited diet of seaweed and shore grasses over the centuries. Though their origins are uncertain, a popular theory holds that these wild ponies are the descendants of horses which swam ashore from the wrecks of Spanish galleons in the 1500s.*

Left: *Chief Fred Bushyhead performs a traditional old style war dance at the AIITCO Pow Wow. Chief Bushyhead, who won the men's old style dancing competition, is one of twenty-nine hereditary chiefs of the Southern Cheyenne tribe of Oklahoma. His regalia features 100 eagle feathers, which have been passed down over generations, and a golden eagle head on his staff, symbolizing his status as chief. The eagle is revered by Indians as a messenger to the Great Spirit.*

Above: *The Maryland Inn, a favorite spot in Annapolis since the days of horse-drawn carriages, is traditionally decorated for Christmas. The inn was constructed in the 1770s.*

Right: *Santa Claus greets spectators at the annual Eastport Yacht Club Christmas Lights Parade in Annapolis. Some seventy sailboats, powerboats, and a Navy patrol boat, all decked out in Christmas lights and decorations, parade around the harbor to the delight of an estimated 15,000 spectators.*

Left: *Another tradition of Christmas in Annapolis is carriage rides through the historic streets. A special attraction is the Chase-Lloyd House, one of the few three-story colonial Georgian mansions in the mid-Atlantic area. Construction was begun in 1769 by Samuel Chase, a signer of the Declaration of Independence, and completed in 1774 by Edward Lloyd IV, a member of the Continental Congress.*

Above: *The Cove, marked by rolling fields of contour ploughing, is one of Garrett County's most impressive sights. This scenic overlook is located along Route 219 north of Accident.*

Left: *Flying Scots rest peacefully before a day of racing at the Deep Creek Lake Yacht Club–Turkey Neck. Established in 1937, this and a neighboring club hold weekend races all summer long. Special invitational regattas attract yachtsmen from as far away as Kentucky and Indiana.*

Following pages: *The frontier spirit is embodied in this weathered cabin in Frederick County. Maryland played a key role in the opening of the West for settlement, offering the Chesapeake & Ohio Canal, the Baltimore & Ohio Railroad, the National Pike, and the National Road, all of which accommodated westward travel.*

Above: *Carrying forth one of the oldest traditions of the Naval Academy, an officer of the U.S. Navy returns to his training grounds to tie the knot at the Academy Chapel. Close friends form the arch of swords. During this week after graduation, there may be as many as ten weddings a day, every hour on the hour.*

Left: *A children's group within Balli D'Italia, an Italian folk art and cultural organization, awaits its cue to dance in the streets of Little Italy during the St. Gabriel's Festival. Little Italy is one of the hundreds of Baltimore's distinct neighborhoods.*

Following pages: *Workmen at the Bethlehem Steel plant at Sparrows Point assist in the open-hearth steelmaking process, which augments the more modern basic oxygen furnace. Home to the largest iron producing blast furnace in the Western Hemisphere, the Sparrows Point plant has an annual raw steel capacity of 5.5 million tons, making it the largest tidewater steel mill in the country. In 1959 the plant saw a peak employment of 30,000; currently some 8,000 men and women are employed there.*

Above: *A sunset cruise caps off a summer vacation in Ocean City. Other popular bayside activities include parasailing, windsurfing, and jet skiing.*

Right: *Canoeing is a favorite way to enjoy the Pocomoke River, which winds its way for sixty miles through the lower Eastern Shore. Named centuries ago by the local Indians for its "black waters," this river is the first in Maryland to be protected as a Wild and Scenic River. Due to its proximity to the temperate Atlantic and bay waters, the Pocomoke environment resembles southern swamps, offering shelter to uncommon flora and fauna, including bald cypress trees with Spanish moss, alligator gar fish, swamp irises and roses, and bald eagles.*

Left: *Fishing along the Chesapeake & Ohio Canal makes for a relaxing summer afternoon near Potomac in Montgomery County. Considered one of the most challenging engineering feats of its day, the canal was constructed between 1828 and 1850 to serve as an economic link to the Midwest. The project was plagued with setbacks and by the time of its completion the canal extended to Cumberland (185 miles from its origin), rising 605 feet with the use of 74 locks.*

Above: Confederate troops hold their ground during a battle with Union forces at Fort Frederick State Park.

Left: Soldiers of the 5th New York regiment Duryee Zouaves suit up during the Living History Weekend at the Ballestone Manor House grounds near Essex in Baltimore County.

Right: The winter serenity of Antietam National Battlefield contrasts sharply with the turmoil of September 17, 1862, when General Robert E. Lee was unsuccessful in his attempts to carry the war effort into the North. Over 23,000 casualties were suffered by both sides during the Battle of Antietam in Washington County, making that day the bloodiest of the Civil War.

Above: Mute swans grace the Chesapeake Bay. Introduced in the United States for zoos, parks and private collections, these majestic birds have since established themselves in the wild, especially along the mid-Atlantic Coast. Their wings are so powerful that they can break a man's leg. Maryland is also home to thousands of tundra swans (also called whistling swans) which migrate to the bay area each fall to escape harsh northern winters.

Left: Acres of water lilies distinguish Lilypons Water Gardens as one of Frederick County's most unusual and colorful attractions. For decades Lilypons has been one of the world's largest suppliers of ornamental fish and aquatic plants.

Above: *Football fans celebrate a Terrapin touchdown during Homecoming at the University of Maryland, College Park. With an enrollment of 37,000 students, it is the state's largest institution of higher education.*

Right: *Winners of the 1987 Miss & Mr. Ocean City Contest pose for one last shot. This annual celebration of summer is held each Saturday at the Ocean Club; winners return for the final Labor Day weekend competition.*

Above: *Winter descends upon Ladew Topiary Gardens, located near Hess in Harford County. Originally a private estate, the gardens are the creation of the late Harvey S. Ladew, who developed the fifteen gardens (covering twenty-two acres) from 1924 to 1971. The focal point of the grounds is Ladew's topiary art (the trimming and training of shrubs, bushes, and trees into ornamental shapes), which has been distinguished by the Garden Club of America as the most outstanding topiary garden in America. Also featured on the property, which has been open to the public since 1976, is his country manor house, filled with English antiques and foxhunting memorabilia.*

Right: *A student from the Maryland Institute College of Art preserves the tranquility of Sherwood Gardens on a rainy weekday. Tucked away in the Baltimore neighborhood of Guilford, the gardens draw thousands of visitors each weekend when spring fever peaks. Originally the private estate of John Sherwood, the gardens have been enjoyed by the public for more than thirty years.*

Following pages: *An Amish farmer sets out to gather a tank full of maple sap on his farm north of Grantsville. The sap is then boiled in the cooking shed, which separates the regular water from the sweet water, yielding thick maple syrup.*

Above: With an uncertain future, skipjacks sail the Chesapeake Bay during a season marked by a poor oyster harvest. Catches of the tasty delicacy have dropped steadily due to over-harvesting and the spread of parasites (harmless to humans) which kill the oysters.

Right: A skipjack captain heads home after a long, cold day on the Chesapeake Bay.

Left: A great blue heron patiently waits for a meal to swim by as the sun sets over Blackwater National Wildlife Refuge in Dorchester County. Unlike most of Blackwater's transient bird population, the great blue heron is a permanent resident which successfully nests in the protected marshes. Over 240 species of birds have been identified on the refuge, which is also home to a variety of mammals, including sika deer, otters and the endangered Delmarva fox squirrel.

Above: Pride of Baltimore II is launched from the Inner Harbor (April 30, 1988) as an estimated crowd of 100,000 cheers her on. Like her predecessor, the Pride of Baltimore, which sank in May 1986 during a sudden squall off Puerto Rico, she will serve as a goodwill ambassador for the city of Baltimore and the state of Maryland, calling on ports around the globe. With an overall length (main boom to jibboom) of 157'3", the Pride of Baltimore II replicates the Baltimore clipper ships of the early nineteenth century, revered for their speed and maneuverability as warships and as cargo ships.

Right: Fireworks explode over Baltimore's Inner Harbor in celebration of a new year.

INDEX

ACKNOWLEDGMENTS

*I would like to thank the following people for their
valuable assistance in my efforts to document Maryland:*

Daniel Ashley
Margaret Avery
Kathleen Bailey
Ted Baldwin
Allison Belgrade
John Bisset
Meg Black
Robert Brenneman
Russell Brenneman
Bob Brugger
Stevens Bunker
Fred Bushyhead
Marion Butler
Brian Butz
Phil Coleman
Keith Davidson
Jesse Davis
Judie Deakins
Ernie Ennis

Joe Ennis
Michael Ennis
Logan Fitzhugh
Doug Gary
Donald Goldsmith
Margaret Hershberger
Robert Hewes
Joan Hill
Joe Hoopes
George Hopkins
Lee Horowitz
Francis Horst
Wilbur Ross Hubbard
Chuck Hughes
Duff Hughes
Sam Hunt
Randy Irwin
Holger Jansson
Robert Joiner

Sam Joiner
Christine Kane
Jim Kiser
James Knaack
Emmett Lanier
Barry Laws
Jennifer Littleton
Chuck Livingston
Hit Man McKay
Max Mosner
Chuck Motsko
Wadie Murphy
Gary Newcomb
John Paradis
Bertha Pinder
Patrick Poloney
Randy Rom
Ed Ross
Jane Rossig

Mardene Rubio
Norman Rukert
Eleanor Schapiro
Michael Schauer
Rick Schnitker
Chip Sheridan
Tom Shouldice
Jeanette Sias
Jim Smith
Jules Smith
Jeff Snyder
Mickey Stenger
Charles Strauss
Mark Thesing
Bill Trautman
Shannon Troxler
Jeff Weissman
Clifton West
Bob Willasch

I would like to especially thank:

*My father, Bob Evans, for providing me the opportunity to assemble
this book, and for his guidance, patience, and encouragement*

*Betsy Hughes, for her thorough text editing, sound advice on
the overall composition of this book, and for her constant enthusiasm*

*John R. Wennersten, Carleton Jones, Lou Rose, and John B. Wiseman
for their enlightening commentaries on Maryland's regions*

Esther Giller, for contributing her marketing expertise

*The staff of GraphTec and The Sheridan Press, for their
commitment to the highest standards of color reproduction and typography*

Brett Bennett, for his elegant map of Maryland